THE LEAF BOOK

Written by ANNE ORANGE
Illustrated by SHARON LERNER

LERNER PUBLICATIONS COMPANY
MINNEAPOLIS, MINNESOTA

To Daniel

AN EARLY NATURE PICTURE BOOK

Copyright © 1975 by Lerner Publications Company

International Standard Book Number: 0-8225-0296-8
Library of Congress Catalog Card Number: 74-12745

2 3 4 5 6 7 8 9 10 85 84 83 82 81 80 79 78 77

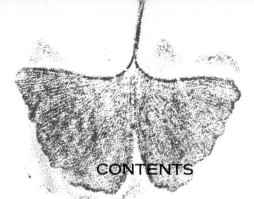

CONTENTS

Do you want to go for a walk? We can walk in the woods.

Look at all the beautiful trees! Let's play a game. We can play it as we walk along. We can try to name the trees.

I know how to name a tree. Do you? The leaves can help you. Pick out a tree. Look at one of its leaves. Look at the shape of the leaf. Look at its size. Look at its edges. Feel it all over.

What tree does your leaf come from?

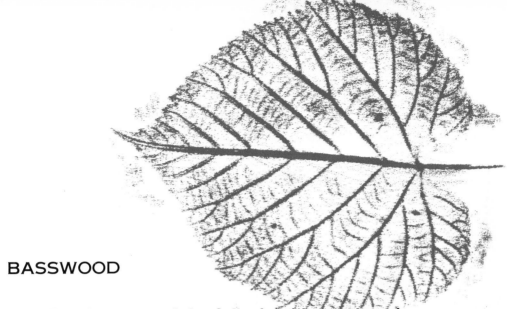

BASSWOOD

The basswood leaf looks like a heart. Look at its edges. Do you see the little teeth?

In the spring, the basswood tree is full of white flowers. Bees buzz around the tree then. They make honey from the sweet flowers. In the fall, the basswood leaves turn yellow.

Some people call the basswood tree by another name. They call it the linden tree.

WHITE OAK

The white oak leaf has many round lobes. These lobes look like little fingers. Each leaf is different. You will never find two white oak leaves that look the same.

The seeds of the oak are called acorns. They are round nuts with smooth shells. Many animals, like squirrels, eat the white oak's acorns. Some people boil the acorns and eat them.

Where does the tree get its name? Look at the bark. It is almost white.

RED OAK

The red oak leaf has lobes like the white oak leaf. But they look different. The red oak's lobes end in sharp points.

The red oak has acorns, too. But they are bitter tasting. Even the squirrels don't like to eat them.

The red oak's leaves change color three times during the year. Now it is summer, and the leaves are green. But they were red in spring. In fall, the leaves change color again. They turn brown.

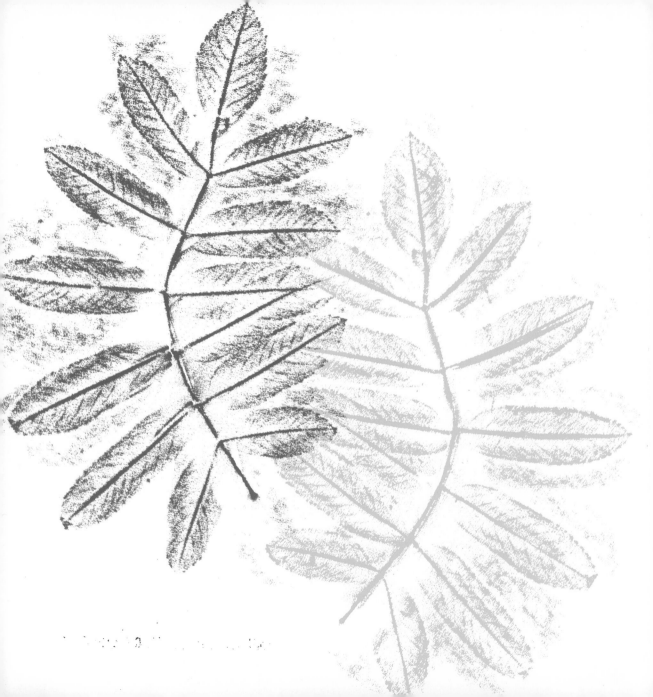

MOUNTAIN ASH

Many leaves grow on one mountain ash branch. They are called **leaflets**. Each leaflet is very small. There are tiny teeth along its edges.

Come back and see this tree in the spring. It is beautiful then. The branches are full of white flowers.

All year long, red berries grow on the mountain ash. Many birds sit in its branches. They like to eat the berries.

13

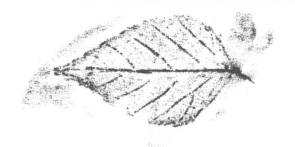

PAPER BIRCH

The paper birch leaf is oval-shaped, like an egg. Feel the leaf. It is very thin. There are small teeth around its edges.

The bark peels off the tree in thin pieces. These pieces of bark look like paper. This is how the tree got its name. But you should not peel the bark off a birch. If too much bark is peeled off a tree, it may die.

This tree has another name, too. Its bark is white. So some people call it the white birch.

COTTONWOOD

The cottonwood leaf is bright shiny green now. In fall, it turns yellow. The leaf is shaped like a triangle. Its edges have little round teeth.

Where did the tree get its name? It is named after its seeds. The seeds are covered with little white hairs. They look like tiny cotton balls.

Watch for them in the spring. They fly in the air when the wind blows. Then it snows cotton.

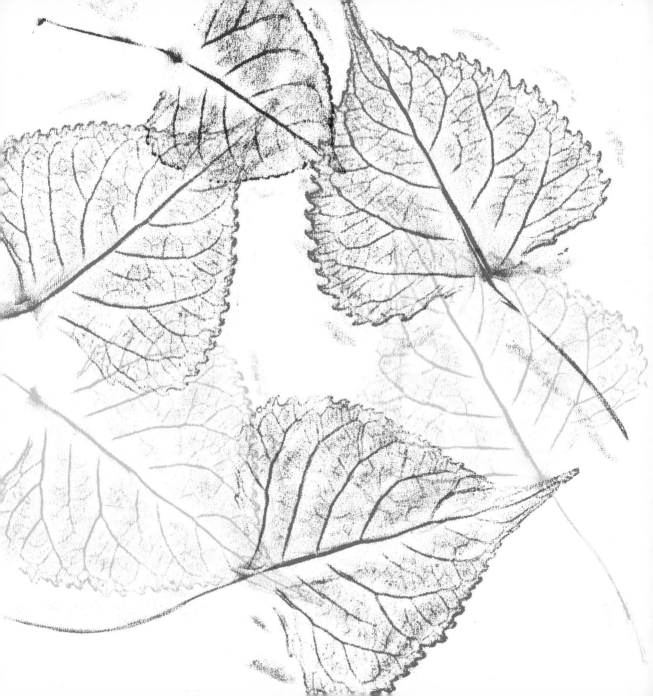

WEEPING WILLOW

The weeping willow leaf is silver green. It is very long and thin. There is a point at the end. Tiny teeth run along the edges.

The branches of the willow drop down to the ground. Let's crawl under them. What a good place to hide!

Willow trees often grow along streams where the ground is wet. This tree needs a lot of water to grow. The willow is pretty in the spring. It is full of flowers then.

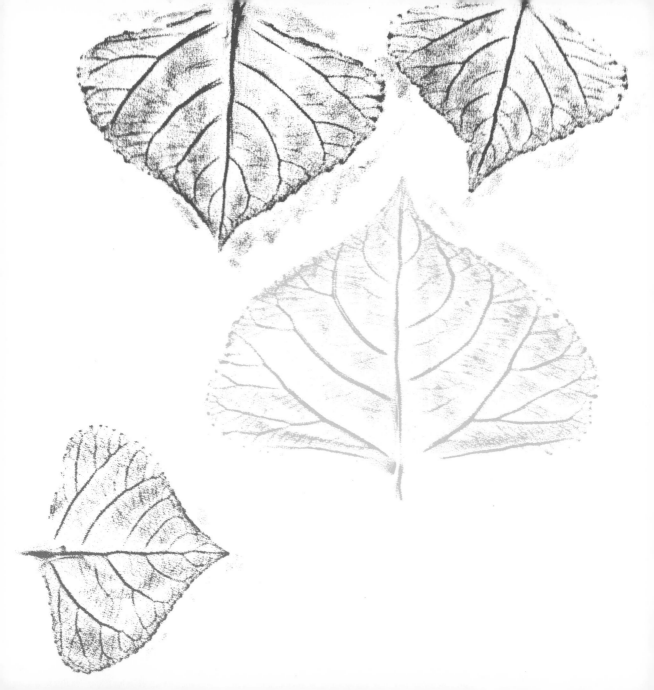

LOMBARDY POPLAR

Does this leaf look like another one that we found? It looks like a cottonwood leaf to me. Poplars and cottonwoods belong to the same tree family.

The Lombardy poplar leaves have flat stems. Because of these flat stems, the leaves wave back and forth in the wind. When this happens, the leaves twinkle in the sunlight.

The Lombardy poplar is a very tall tree. It is also very thin. Its branches grow upward. They point to the sky.

SUGAR MAPLE

The sugar maple leaf is dark green. It has five lobes. The lobes have pointed ends.

You should see this tree in the fall. It is full of color then. Some leaves turn red. Others turn yellow or orange.

We get something good to eat from the sugar maple tree. Can you guess what? Maple syrup!

The wood of the sugar maple is very hard. It is used in making furniture.

SILVER MAPLE

The silver maple leaf looks very much like the sugar maple leaf. They both have five lobes. But look close. The lobes of the silver maple leaf are longer.

The top of this leaf is light green. Turn the leaf over. Now you know how the tree got its name. The back of the leaf is silver! In fall, the leaf turns yellow.

The seeds of both the silver maple and the sugar maple grow in clusters on the trees' branches. These seeds look like tiny wings.

ELM

The elm leaf is oblong, or egg-shaped. It has little teeth running along its edges. There is a point at the end of it.

You see elm trees growing all over. They are popular trees. Many grow along city streets. Sometimes they grow so high they make a roof over the street. Elm trees also grow to be very old. Some elms are over 100 years old.

27

GINKGO

The ginkgo leaf is shaped like a fan. Some of the leaves are very tiny. Others are big. The big leaves have short cuts in their centers.

The ginkgo leaf is a beautiful green now. In fall, it turns bright yellow. The ginkgo is a very old tree. Ginkgo trees first grew in the gardens of China and Japan a long time ago.

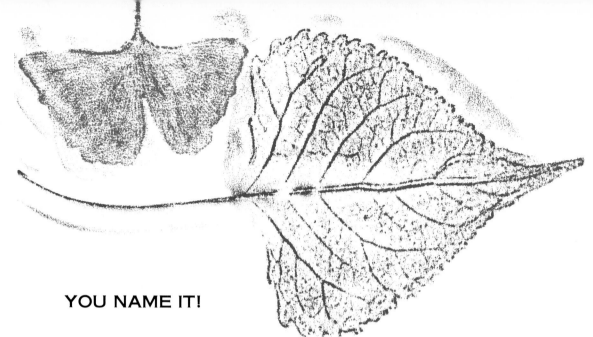

YOU NAME IT!

Now you know how to name a tree. Its leaves will tell you. You have learned about many trees in this book. A lot of them can be found near your home. Look around you! What leaves can you find?

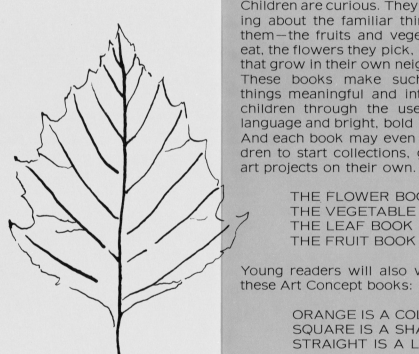

Children are curious. They enjoy learning about the familiar things around them—the fruits and vegetables they eat, the flowers they pick, or the trees that grow in their own neighborhoods. These books make such everyday things meaningful and interesting to children through the use of simple language and bright, bold illustrations. And each book may even inspire children to start collections, gardens, or art projects on their own.

THE FLOWER BOOK
THE VEGETABLE BOOK
THE LEAF BOOK
THE FRUIT BOOK

Young readers will also want to see these Art Concept books:

ORANGE IS A COLOR
SQUARE IS A SHAPE
STRAIGHT IS A LINE